People Skills for Business

Winning Social Skills That Put You Ahead of the Competition

Melissa Contreras

First Printing, 2013
ISBN-13: 978-1490381442
Printed in the United States of America

Income Disclaimer

This document contains business strategies, marketing methods and other business advice that, regardless of my own results and experience, may not produce the same results (or any results) for you. I make absolutely no guarantee, expressed or implied, that by following the advice below you will make any money or improve current profits, as there are several factors and variables that come into play regarding any given business.

Primarily, results will depend on the nature of the product or business model, the conditions of the marketplace, the experience of the individual, and situations and elements that are beyond your control.

As with any business endeavor, you assume all risk related to investment and money based on your own discretion and at your own potential expense.

Liability Disclaimer

By reading this document, you assume all risks associated with using the advice given below, with a full understanding that you, solely, are responsible for anything that may occur as a result of putting this information into action in any way, and regardless of your interpretation of the advice.

You further agree that our company cannot be held responsible in any way for the success or failure of your business as a result of the information presented below. It is your responsibility to conduct your own due diligence regarding the safe and successful operation of your business if you intend to apply any of our information in any way to your business operations.

Terms of Use

You are given a non-transferable, "personal use" license to this product. You cannot distribute it or share it with other individuals.

Also, there are no resale rights or private label rights granted when purchasing this document. In other words, it's for your own personal use only.

People Skills for Business

Winning Social Skills That
Put You Ahead of the Competition

Table of Contents

CHAPTER 1

People Skills: What Are They? How Can Having Them Be Good For Business?

People Skills 101: The Business Essentials

Getting up close and personal with clients, professional associates, and employees is a simple matter, really. To create lasting bonds and that all-important sense of trust, all one needs is a few people skills.

When we exercise people skills, we are enacting behaviors designed to bring people closer to us. In the workplace, we are exercising these skills constantly – whether we know it or not. In addition to people or soft skills, we also bring our occupational or hard skills to the office. These hard skills generally lend themselves to the type of work that we do, helping us forge solid businesses. Soft skills lend themselves to this path, smoothing the way for us as we grow our ventures, but we also use them quite a bit in our social lives and dealings outside business.

Here are some of the abilities that are among the important people skills that we take to the office:

- Effective communication
- Ability to establish rapport
- Conflict resolution
- Negotiation
- Persuasion
- Stress management
- Strategic problem solving and planning
- Team building

When you sharpen these abilities, you are enhancing your emotional IQ, expanding your general ability to form business relationships and even brightening your personal persona, heightening your own personal brands of confidence and sociability.

Building strong relationships with members of your team and clients can lead to great things, and when you take the necessary steps to strengthen your social skills, you are certain to make your life a happier place. Future contracts and transactions – whether they take place in your place of business or at home – will go smoother and you'll certainly feel the effects when they improve your attitude and even your physical health.

Because strong interpersonal relationship skills have been linked with so many significant benefits, they have long been studied by wise men and scholars throughout human history.

The Goods: How People Skills Enhance the Realm of Business

Since the dawn of civilization, humans have been gregarious creatures. We learned long ago that our lives are simpler and more successful when we help each other out from time to time. In our modern world, it's become possible to live without substantial help from the community, but if we want to establish a happy family and a successful career, we have little choice but to learn how to effectively communicate with others.

When we are able to create strong, positive relationships with our clients, suppliers, business partners and associates, our careers will certainly flourish. If you run your own business, or deal with clients, investors, suppliers and employees on a regular basis, it is absolutely essential to develop strong people skills.

Other people will notice when you have the ability to deftly handle yourself in any situation, and this positive perception can lead to you getting what you want – the heavyweight client, the hefty raise, affordable loan conditions, a conflict resolution that works in your favor, the office teammates of your choosing – under just as many different circumstances.

Your improved people skills will lend itself to higher amounts of confidence, charisma, and even Zen in the face of a stressful workday. Your newfound communicative clarity will allow others to obtain a good understanding of what you think and expect, and, thanks to your startlingly effective problem-solving abilities, your coworkers will look to you for leadership.

Of course, enhancing your people skills isn't about manipulating others and getting your way all the time. Improved interpersonal skills will win people over to your side, but not everything is a battle to the finish. The most important result of a superior emotional IQ is the trust it creates between you and your associates.

The trust people will have in you is what will drive all your future business endeavors together: when clients sense that you have their interests at heart, they'll keep coming back for more.

Heightened confidence correlates strongly with a positive attitude, which in turn is related to the ability to find solutions for even the toughest problems. When others notice your friendly, solution-oriented persona, they'll look forward to doing business with you. This kind of draw should be enough to make anyone want to build better interpersonal skills. After all, when your face-to-face interactions with clientele and partners are enhanced, your company will grow right alongside them.

On a similar note, business owners would greatly enhance their bottom line by hiring people with strong interpersonal skills. Such employees are to be treasured – a team of friendly, positive people will attract a better kind of business.

CHAPTER 2

Active Listening: What Does the Client Really Want?

Are You Actually Listening? Learn to Tell the Difference between Passive, Attentive, and Active Listening

If you're not talking, it doesn't mean that you must be listening. If people around you complain that you aren't listening, it means that you don't fully comprehend what they are trying to communicate. Of course, this problem might not be completely your fault, depending on a number of factors. If a coworker isn't communicating effectively, your best efforts at listening might not result in an understanding. However, if you don't know how to listen effectively, odds are that you haven't been putting enough effort into your conversations – doing so is more common than you might think.

There is a substantial difference between merely hearing and really listening. Hearing describes our ability to perceive sounds, but listening suggests that we're using our brains to make an attempt at understanding what's being said.

More than that, there are three main types of listening, involving three different levels of perception:

- **Passive listening:** When we are listening passively, we're not entirely focused on the words coming at us from the outside. We may be distracted – sending a text, writing an email, readjusting calendar entries, planning the rest of the day – and perhaps are only pretending to listen, largely ignoring the message in question. Passive listeners are probably picking out select phrases, mistakenly believing that these summarize the communication.

- **Attentive listening:** This involves more participation on our part. We are processing more of what someone else has to say, picking up on facts and the general emotions behind the message. By listening attentively, we can come to a relative understanding with someone else. Speakers will pick up on an attentive listener's apparent focus via posture and demeanor.

- **Active listening:** We have reached the Holy Grail of paying attention when we are listening actively. We are giving our complete attention to a speaker's message, physically displaying our interest, deciding where we should request further information, and showing how dedicated we are to creating an understanding. Active listening is an active process – we are a dynamic part of a conversation, taking time and brainpower to understand a communication and actively contribute to the topic at hand.

Listen Actively to Strengthen Your Business

Some estimate that we fail to absorb about 70 percent of the communications hurdled at us on a daily basis. Often we zone out in the middle of a communication, thinking we know how it's going to end, and we begin to prepare a response before we've received all the necessary information. Although it seems counterproductive, our minds can't help but work faster than our ears can receive information, so jumping to conclusions is almost a natural action.

Of course, jumping to conclusions can be problematic in business situations. When you practice active listening, on the other hand, you can help your business run more smoothly in a number of different ways. When you aren't coming to false conclusions based on information gaps, you can improve your business in the following manner:

- Increased management response and effectiveness
- Higher quality of customer relations

- Reduced conflict
- Less customer complaints
- Improved levels of customer satisfaction
- Healthier, friendlier workplace
- Improved negotiations with clients and partners

When you don't practice active listening, you may be leaving the fate of your business to chance. However, when you attune yourself to the opinions, wants, needs, and drives of others, you create the opportunity for all-around better business practices.

12 Ways to Become an Active Listener

When we listen *actively*, we are putting forth a conscious effort to absorb what a speaker is attempting to communicate. Although simple, the process is multifaceted and can differ slightly for each of us. Practicing these 12 methods of active listening will bring even the most inattentive listener to heel.

1. **Face the Speaker:** Display your attention and openness by sitting or standing facing the speaker. Positioning yourself in such a way will allow you to look directly at the speaker, and it will also let him know he is being heard. When you sit with your shoulders or crossed legs facing someone, they are more likely to feel that you are engaged in the conversation. This is a fact most easily understood by considering the antithesis: if a friend or coworker turns his head toward you, but keeps his body facing forty-five degrees in another direction, you are

unlikely to feel that he is really engaged in whatever you have to say. When he swivels his chair to face you, on the other hand, you're more likely to feel comfortable and encouraged to speak. Facing a speaker is a subtle way of displaying your interest, but not one that will go unnoticed. Of course, continuing to face away from someone who is speaking is likely to cast a negative light on the communication.

2. **Establish a Friendly Eyeline:** The importance of maintaining friendly – but not overpowering – eye contact cannot be underestimated. A speaker feels encouraged to continue when a listener is meeting their eyes. As a listener, this is the easiest way to express interest up for discussion. Of course, too much eye contact – also known as staring – can be problematic, making the speaker feel uncomfortable. It's natural to break eye contact every once in a while to avoid creating tension and even to ponder about the subject matter of the conversation. Try to maintain eye contact about 70 to 80 percent of the time.

3. **Eliminate External Distractions:** Exercising environmental control over external distractions is important in our modern world. We tend to carry around various devices that love nothing more than to ding and sing and vibrate whenever we receive an email, text, phone call, tweet, or Facebook message. Since such noises represent a kind of reward, our brains sometimes develop the habit of sending a shot of dopamine to our neural reward pathways, creating

the urge to pick up the device right away and obtain that reward. Avoid this altogether by turning these devices off or completely silencing them. There's nothing more disheartening than to be interrupted by someone else's Smartphone, and, worse, to have a listener show you that their text message is more important than whatever you have to say. Don't be that listener – eliminate potential distractions in advance.

4. **Soothe Internal Distractions:** These diversions can include feelings of hunger or thirst, an urge to use the restroom, or emotions related to your personal life, all of which can be incredibly problematic when you are trying to play the attentive listener. To avoid a bad situation, attend to any physical needs before any scheduled meetings. Of course, this won't always be possible. Luckily, there are still a few options left to you: commit yourself to overcoming internal distractions, or, if this just isn't possible, request to move the meeting to a time when are able to comfortably proceed.

5. **Exhibit 'I'm Listening' Body Language:** Outside of facing the speaker and establishing eye contact, you can use your bodily communications to send a relaxed, interested, and encouraging vibe. This involves keeping your arms uncrossed, giving the occasional nod, and leaning forward slightly. Your nods don't have to indicate agreement – only that you are listening intently.

6. **Don't Interrupt:** You know you want to, but it's important not to interrupt. Many of us listen to part of a communication, and, before we hear all of it, interrupt because we think we have thought of a solution or witty reply. However, if you haven't heard the entire communication, you haven't received the entire picture. By letting others have their say, you can come up with a better solution (if a solution is what's needed) and a wittier reply. Not only that, but you will express empathy and attention toward your clients and colleagues, who will likely do the same for you. Merely listening can soothe an angry customer, smooth rough communications, and create an opening for a productive discussion about even the most controversial of subjects (sometimes, all people want is to be heard). Keep your opinions, witticisms, and solutions to yourself until after a speaker has spoken.

7. **Avoid Making Judgments:** When you keep an open mind, you encourage others to do the same for you. Prejudging a person's message before it has been fully communicated can be problematic, leaving you with a muddled version of the truth. Avoid jumping to conclusions by paying attention to the speaker's body language, emotional state, and the facts being communicated. Remember the saying about what happens when you assume (don't know it? look it up!).

8. **Embrace Silence:** This is one of the best ways to avoid interrupting a communication. When a speaker seems to have finished, allow a beat or two of silence

to pass between you and really establish whether he has said all he plans to say. He may simply be pondering his next sentence, so be respectful of his right to mull over his thoughts. If you accidentally interrupt him in this manner, he may get the wrong idea – it may seem as if you were only waiting for your turn to give an opinion rather than actually listening.

9. **Don't Make It About You:** Showing someone that you know what they mean by exclaiming, "Me, too!" and launching into a personal story to underscore your point can backfire. Interrupting with this kind of parable may leave the impression that you are not actually listening, and that you seem to want to spend the entire conversation in the spotlight – obviously not the best impression to make.

10. **Ask Questions But Don't Interrupt:** This can be tricky, but, with a little practice, you'll get the hang of it. You can show your level of interest by asking intelligent questions, but avoid asking closed, yes-or-no questions. An open-ended question – "I'd really like to know more about that, can you tell me how exactly that works?" – will supply you with essential information and enhance the quality of the conversation at the same time. When the answer is only "yes" or "no," you won't learn as much or seem as interested. Asking a question tends to be somewhat of an interruption, so be sure not to ask too many questions or to interrupt in a manner that disrupts another's train of thought or seems rude.

11. **Encourage Continued Speech:** As you listen, demonstrate that you would like the speaker to continue through your body language and subtle verbal cues. These verbal appendages should encourage rather than interrupt, so keep them simple: use statements like "I see," "hmm," "uh-huh," or "that's interesting." Remember to give a few nods throughout the conversation as well. Don't overdo it, however, or you may appear false or sycophantic.

12. **Reflect Back Upon the Speaker:** When a speaker has finished, make sure you really do have a good handle on his words by paraphrasing what he just said. Doing so will allow the speaker to confirm your understanding or clarify what you didn't fully grasp. One way to reflect back upon the speaker is to say something like, "If I understand correctly, you think that.... Would that be a fair statement?" or "I believe what you're saying is that.... Am I right about that?"

An active listener is able to exert effort and come to an understanding of what is being communicated. When a listener is active, the speaker feels heard – because he is. Although the act of active listening is largely about the speaker, the listener still benefits in many ways from the outcome. After all, active listening is more than mere listening – it's a fundamental tool for relationship-building.

LISTEN: Establishing Strong Active Listening Habits

The necessary attitude and skills required in active listening can be summarized in one memorable acronym – LISTEN.

Look: Face the speaker so you can view him directly, engage in friendly eye contact, and show with your body that you are absorbing his words.

Inquire: To gather further information, establish clarity, and express your interest, ask intelligent questions.

Summarize: Confirm your understanding by paraphrasing the message and repeating it back to the speaker. This important step will allow you to avoid confusion that may result in preventable complications.

Turn off Distractions: Silence or switch off all electronic devices, dim your computer screen, and otherwise make an attempt to control any exterior sources of distraction.

Encourage: Express your interest in the topic at hand with small verbal cues and encouraging gestures.

Neutralize Your Emotions and Preexisting Opinions: Make an attempt to come to every conversation with a clean, unbiased slate. Remember, you're participating in this communication and making at attempt at active listening because you want to better understand another's point of view, which may well mean that you're not going to agree with that view. If you allow yourself to become swept up in judgments and personal beliefs, you may miss an excellent opportunity to do business. Keep your opinions to yourself until it's time to express them, but, while listening, it's best to neutralize your feelings and attend to the message being communicated.

> *Remember! Active listeners manage to perform the following actions:*
>
> - **Establish good rapport with others**
> - **Attack issues, NOT people**
> - **Work in teams comfortably**
> - **Listen more than talk**
> - **Express genuine interest in understanding what others have to say**

CHAPTER 3

Using and Reading Body Language to Your Advantage

Decoding Body Language's Best Kept Secrets

Our Bodies Can Communicate

No matter how much you love to talk, approximately 80 percent of what you are communicating is being conveyed through body language alone – that's how important it is to those around you.

Listeners are taking in your tone of voice in addition to watching your eye movements, facial expressions, body position, and gestures, which often have a tone of their own. All of these things – how you're standing, whether you use your arms and hands, facial expressions – communicate an overriding message to those around us. This message is more important than anything we say and will make or break the impression you leave with others.

By now, it should be apparent why business professionals simply can't go without learning the ins and outs of body language. When you learn the effects of body language, you can better control the message you send to others.

In addition to exhibiting stronger body language, you can also learn how to consciously read the nonverbal cues of others. Much of the time, people allow their body language to communicate to us without any conscious effort, and, as such, it provides a wealth of clues that can be helpful during any communication.

Making a Strong First Impression

How do you want to be remembered? Not many people would say they wish others to think them timid and deceitful. In our society, a firm handshake is one of the best ways to communicate our strong, confident personalities. Provide a flimsy, weak handshake and many will come to the immediately conclusion that you lack confidence or conviction.

In addition to a strong shake, an awareness of what your body language conveys to those around you is an essential part of making an excellent first impression. Making eye contact, speaking in a clear, concise manner, and displaying open arm and hand motions are among the best techniques for creating a favorable first impression. When you can make others feel good about meeting you, you set the tone for future interactions.

How Body Language Sets the Tone

We may not notice it, but body language lays the groundwork for how people perceive each other and how well their interactions will go. Trained, professional speakers use body language in a conscious effort to shape how their communications will be received. Luckily, these tricks are not difficult to learn.

Our posture – whether good or bad – sends out signals about our level of confidence. Even if you're not feeling confident, you can fake it with excellent posture.

If you wish to convey a sense of urgency, make excessive hand or arm gestures. If, on the opposite end of the spectrum, you wish to set a soothing tone, make slow, minimal gestures.

Again, making direct eye contact is one way to demonstrate that you are listening, interested, and open. However, don't overdo it as staring makes most of us fairly uncomfortable.

Much like speechwriters pay special attention to *le mot juste* ("the right word"), speech givers must pay careful attention to what the body is communicating. To communicate properly, you must be sure that your body isn't saying something unintentional.

The Secret of Body Language

Body language cannot be faked – at least, not entirely. The combined use of self-awareness and self-control will allow you to minimize the negative emotions you send out, but if, say, you're feeling especially angry, that is likely to show through no matter what you do.

Take the story of Jeff, for example, who had been working at his job, an especially demanding position, for more than 25 years and often felt tired. Throughout the last few years, his employer had been steadily hiring many young employees, and the generation gap between then and Jeff was becoming increasingly apparent.

When these young employees failed to meet his expectations, he couldn't help but feel irate. He viewed their mistakes as careless, and, although he never mentioned it, his anger was palpable. His younger coworkers knew to steer clear of Jeff whenever he began clenching his hands or squinting his eyes.

In turn, Jeff could sense that his coworkers were avoiding him. Eventually, he decided to sign up for a communications course that taught students new techniques for exercising control over their own body language. He learned through the class that, no matter how hard he fought to hide his emotions, his feelings were so strong that they were evident to some degree to those around him. Instead of trying to hide negative feelings and allowing them to continue to affect him, he should instead try to work them out in a constructive manner.

The truth is that we never have complete control over the messages we send to others any more than we can control the emotions we feel in any given situation. Still, there are many ways in which we can manage what our bodies communicate to others.

Common Body Language Tell-Alls

According to a University of Pennsylvania study, body language leaves more of a lasting impression than anything we have to say. The same study found that when people form an impression, 55 percent of that impression is based on posture, gestures, and body movements, 38 percent is created by tone of voice, and 7 percent is drawn from verbal communication.

It's clear that if we master our movements, we can contribute greatly to what people think of us. But what about interpreting what the body language of other people is telling us?

Interpreting Common Gestures and Stances

Here are a few common examples of body language and what these gestures communicate:

- **Crossed Arms:** A man with his arms cross over his chest is in effect creating a barrier between himself and other people. This common gesture is often a subconscious way of keeping others at bay, but it communicates a strong message to those who can see you: "I'm shutting you out."

- **Eye Contact:** By maintaining eye contact, we communicate our interest and attention. Again, however, eye contact that is too overwhelming can suggest the opposite of respectful listening and can even communicate certain hostility.

- **Lack of Eye Contact:** This is taken by most people as sign of indifference or pessimism. Lowered eyes may communicate timidity and averted eyes can suggest disbelief.

- **Good Posture:** This is the ultimate display of confidence. Clasping the hands loosely behind the back or over the stomach contributes an air of relaxation to this confidence.

- **Rapid Hand and Arm Gestures:** These are typically a sign of excitement, enthusiasm, or urgency. They can, however, represent too much of a good thing; overusing them may look a little strange.

Keeping an Open Mind

Each of our gestures and postures makes its own suggestions. When we attempt to shape others' impressions of us, it's important to understand what each gesture is communicating. Similarly, it's important to see what our associates are communicating to us with their body language. A smile is the universal symbol of happiness and welcome. Likewise, a clenched fist usually means tension or trouble. On the other hand, many examples of body language can be easily misunderstood. For example:

- **Crossed Arms:** These usually represent a defensive posture, but some people are simply more comfortable with their arms crossed. For example, one common way of keeping warm is by crossing the arms over the chest.

- **Fidgeting:** A person who is restlessly tapping her foot or twisting the rings on her fingers may appear nervous, but she may also merely be unconscious of what she is doing.

- **Restless Movement:** When someone appears unable to sit still, he may be impatient, but he may also be suffering from a pair of uncomfortable shoes or having eaten a bad egg at lunch.

In the case of ambiguous body language, it's typically a good idea not to read too much into it. Whatever you do, don't make judgments. Rather than coming to finite conclusions, remember that it's always better to treat body language as one part of a multifaceted communications picture.

At the same time, we must be vigilant about what our bodies may be communicating to others. It might be comfortable to cross our arms over our chests, but then how will a potential client see you? Most likely she'll perceive it as something negative, which may make her wary of working with you.

Body Language in a Business Meeting: 10 Must-Use Techniques

1. Put Emotions in Check

Transform you body language by observing and acknowledging the emotions behind your desired communication. If your emotions begin to get the better of you, take a deep breath before pushing forward. Communicate certain feelings – happiness, enthusiasm – by really feeling them. Take a moment before you begin to cultivate genuine positive feelings.

2. Create an Open Stance

By standing with the feet at hip-width, you create a welcoming, open stance. When your feet are too close together, you may appear reserved or uncomfortable. On the other hand, when the feet are spread too wide, this position may communicate aggression. There is balance and grounding in a hip-width stance.

3. Keep Arms to the Sides

It's important to be aware of arm movement, as too much can reduce credibility and inhibit an audience. If arms are closed, they communicate aggression or closed-mindedness. Open arms, left to the sides of the body, indicate open-mindedness and a relaxed nature. However, this position can be difficult to maintain and takes a little getting used to, so be sure to practice.

4. Open the Palms

Our hands communicate quite a bit of emotional information. Fidgeting hands lend themselves to nervousness, clenched fists represent anger or aggression, and tightly clasped hands can indicate insecurity. Portray confidence, openness, and relaxation by keeping your palms open.

5. Create Confident Posture

A straight spine, all the way through the neck, is the best possible indicator of confidence. Display yours by throwing back your shoulders and opening your chest. Again, arms should be relaxed at the sides. From this position, the world will look like an entirely different place.

6. Throw the Shoulders Back

While slumped shoulders represent insecurity or fatigue, thrown-back shoulders are the epitome of confidence and security.

7. Lean into the Conversation

When you lean – ever so slightly – into a conversation, you give the impression that you are trusting and trustworthy, open, and willing to make a connection. If you are the listener, you will make the speaker feel heard, understood, and valued. Leaning in slightly can have a massive impact on establishing rapport and trust.

8. Relax the Facial Muscles

Humans perceive quite a bit of information concerning emotional state based on the way our eyes, nose, cheeks, mouth, and forehead move. So, to better impress clients and colleagues, keep all of these facial features as relaxed as possible, allowing others to see how tranquil and approachable you are. If there is tension in your face – crinkling the forehead, narrowing the eyes, clenching the jaw – you may be unwittingly suggesting aggression.

9. Smile

Show off your positive attitude in the best possible manner – with a smile. A constant smile will most likely feel awkward and seem false, so it's better to flash the occasional smile instead, which is what probably will feel more natural to you anyway. Doing so will help you keep the tension out of your face and a light in your eyes. Be sure to skip the Botox – smiles have the most power over others when they move over the entire face, lifting the cheeks into apples and crinkling the skin around the eyes.

10. Soft Eyes

Soft eyes keep you from missing the forest, but they also convey the positive emotions you are feeling. Relax the muscles around the eyes – as opposed to squinting - and focus on the speaker or audience in front of you for the best effect. There's a reason why your eyes are the window to your soul – people pick up on what you're feeling by gazing into them.

CHAPTER 4

Improve Your Public Speaking Practices

As a business leader, you are left with little choice but to get over any fear of public speaking you may be harboring. After all, public speaking is a necessity for everyone, especially business owners and members of management. Still, it can be tough – many studies have shown that people fear public speaking more than they fear death.

The act of public speaking is often a mandatory aspect of your repertoire as a business leader and can materialize in a number of different ways: in the form of an employee pep talk, investment pitch, or meeting with your partners. You can't avoid speaking publically, but there are many methods to help you both quell anxiety and improve your ability to impress a crowd.

Preparation and Practice

Public speaking is like anything else – the level of practice and preparation directly correlates with a speaker's level of success. Preparation has the added benefit of boosting confidence; for public speakers, there are few worse things than heading out onto a stage before a large crowd completely unprepared.

What defines preparation? It's simple, really: being prepared is a matter of knowing and understanding your subject matter well enough to speak about it in an unaffected manner. In other words, you don't have to read your speech word-for-word from note cards because you've mastered the subject and can discuss it naturally. There's no need for memorization, either – many of the best speeches differ slightly from their written forms. You're prepared when you know what you're talking about and have a plan for approaching the subject matter.

There's another reason why you needn't memorize your speech, especially if you have high levels of anxiety: Disruptions and unexpected situations are bound to arise, and if they cause you to lose your train of thought, you may be left fumbling for what you were going to say next. When an audience witnesses this kind of internal conflict, your credibility as an authority is tarnished.

Such a situation is easily avoided by preparation. Rather than memorizing every word, familiarize yourself with your main points – know them backwards and forwards. Write cues for each main point on your note cards to serve as points of reference. You'll be able to look down at them and remind yourself what you were planning to say next. Note cards or slides should act as a guide to a predetermined structure rather than spelling out exactly what you want to say.

Lastly, be sure that any props you plan to use are in working order before your speech begins. Make sure you know what you're doing as well. Having your audience wait for you to learn to use a projector is not only distracting for them but can also become irritating.

Strengthen Your Grip: Your Handshake

Before a speaking engagement with clients or potential investors, boost your business credibility by making a firm first impression. In our society, a strong handshake speaks volumes and comes before all other business interactions – it is the first impression of first impressions. We can't help but make judgments on character and confidence based on the handshake, so it's important to strengthen yours. The following tips are certain to improve your grip:

- **Make the First Offer:** When you extend your hand first, you put yourself in a kind of power position. Not only that, but you are proffering your interest, openness, and confidence.

- **Show Good Form:** Extend an outstretched hand, thumb up, fingers straight and together, and slide to into the other person's until they touch. Pump twice – no more, no less.

- **It's in the Grip:** The only proper handshake is a firm one. A strong, firm grip communicates sincerity and professionalism, whereas a limp grip can come off as weak and standoffish. A barely-touching handshake is equally disagreeable.

- **Don't Overdo It:** Shaking a hand isn't a battle of Titans. Be firm, but don't grip so tightly as to cause another person pain. Likewise, pump the other person's arm firmly and deliberately, but not in a rapid or overbearing manner. Be especially careful when shaking the hands of an older generation, who may suffer from carpal tunnel, and be sensitive to the fact that anyone may have a skin allergy or fragile bones.

- **Handshake Equality:** These rules apply to equally to women in the modern business environment. We no longer live in a world where it is not proper for a woman to extend her hand first, and a woman is not expected to act dainty and weak. Ladies benefit equally from a firm grip and a smart handshake.

The Power of Storytelling to Engage an Audience

In the public speaking arsenal, there is no greater weapon than the story. After all, who doesn't love a good story? Stories can be worked into a speech in order to capture audience attention, bring up a new point, or simply as a funny aside to reward an attentive crowd. If you're dealing with a particularly difficult concept, use storytelling as a device to help people better understand the points you wish to make.

When you find yourself at a podium, it's most likely because you've been tasked with selling ideas or persuading a group of people to do something. To sell or sway your audience you must first connect with them emotionally, and a story is the perfect way to forge such a connection.

Consider your business dealings and you're certain to come up with a range of clever stories that will delight an audience. How, then, do you go about delivering one?

- **Start at the Beginning:** Tell your audience who you are, why you're speaking to them, and why they should trust what you are saying.

- **Get Personal:** When you share a personal story you're inviting listeners into your world, demonstrating openness and trust and inviting them to do the same. By revealing a personal flaw or a past mistake you immediately make yourself relatable and approachable.

- **Inspire:** Show your audience the possibilities behind what you're selling, using your words to really involve all of their senses and creating a vivid scene. Remember that the best way to truly inspire is to remain authentic. There's no need to dress up your story with false optimism or fake antidotes.

Paraphrasing: The Ultimate Tool to Establish Rapport and Avoid Misunderstandings

Eventually it'll be time to answer any questions your audience may have in regards to your speech. Recall that paraphrasing is one of your greatest tools to gain clarity.

After each question is asked, summarize it for the person asking. In this manner, you can ensure that you and your audience are on a level plane of understanding. Paraphrasing is the simplest method to learn whether you've correctly interpreted a question.

If, for example, you've just given a speech to a group of potential clients and one asks you to go back over the part concerning media marketing, you might say, "Do you mean the five aspects of our social media marketing strategy?" By paraphrasing as well as adding additional specificity you force this potential client to make his question clear to you. This way you'll both be on the same page.

Dress for Success

If you're preparing to stand before a group of clients, coworkers, employees, or potential business investors, you've got to dress the part. Namely, you must project authority and stability. So what do you wear to accomplish such a feat?

Much like body language, our clothing gives others clues on how to perceive us. Unlike body language, however, we have a huge level of control over what we convey through clothing.

In a business setting, people expect a certain degree of conservatism as well as relative sameness. It conveys a sense of "safeness" to others and you actually are perceived as less risky to do business with. You can still make sure your personality comes through though, with a splash of color or a subtle accessory. But until your authority is established with your client and in the industry it might be best to play it safe with the way you present yourself.

Grooming is of equal importance. Ladies should style their hair neatly and wear their makeup in a classic style – unless your specific line of business expects otherwise, of course. Men should also make sure that their hair looks presentable. Both should take care that fingernails are clean and neat, as our hands do a lot of "talking" during meetings.

Strike a Positive Note with Confident Body Language

Cool, Calm and Collected Win the Day

Even with practice and preparation, a little game day anxiety may be inevitable. If you feel the panic start to set in, whatever you do, don't let it take over.

If a little voice in the back of your mind pipes up with accusations and put-downs, silence it with positive self-talk. Reassure yourself that you're well prepared for this presentation, and that you're going to do just fine.

Another preparation technique, regularly practiced by world-class athletes, is positive visualization. Find a quiet place to sit and visualize how your speech will go. See it going perfectly, and don't forget to imagine how impressed and persuaded the audience is to hear what you have to say. Try to make the vision as detailed as possible. Practice this technique every day leading up to your speech as a kind of exercise. Do it again just before speaking.

By using these techniques to quell your fear, you'll be better able to appear calm and confident to your audience. Once you have your emotions somewhat under control, you'll be able to exercise what you know about body language to display your authority. Here are a few aspects of body language that are especially important when giving a speech:

- **Claiming Your Space:** Every speaker is allotted a certain amount of platform from which to address the audience – use yours wisely. Show that you are comfortable before a crowd by commanding that space to the best of your ability. Take a few steps forward or to the side as you speak, making eye contact and engaging with those in the vicinity. Don't move so much that you distract from your message, but let your audience know who has the floor.

- **Staying Open, Making Defined Gestures:** Many of us can't help but use our hands when we speak, and such gestures become very important in a public setting. Begin your speech with an open stance, with arms to the sides. It can be difficult - even for actors - to stand like this, but displaying openness in all directions is important. Keep hand and arm gestures to a minimum, and, when you do exercise them, use strong, smooth motions.

- **Soft Eyes, Expressive Face:** Much of your meaning will be derived from your facial expression. If people normally find your face difficult to read, you may want to practice conveying a friendly openness in the mirror before the big speech. Too much facial expression may come off as fake, and too little will leave listeners cold.

- **Voice Monitoring:** When it comes to public speaking, your voice is as important a tool as any. It can be used to convey emotion, draw the crowd into a story, or bore them to tears. If you have difficulty convey expressiveness through voice inflections, consider working with a speech coach. Doing so will improve what your audience hears.

Squash Self-Consciousness

If you're one of the people who fears public speaking more than death, you may believe that other people can see how uncomfortable you are at the podium. This, however, is highly unlikely. Unless someone in the crowd knows you well – as well as, say, your mother – your fear probably isn't as obvious as you think.

Focusing on who can see your knees knocking, on the other hand, will only cause your anxiety to build. When you get going, don't make too much of small mistakes. Rather than blundering over a stuttered word, simply smile and move on as if it doesn't bother you. Your obvious discomfort before the crowd may affect listeners negatively. If you don't *appear* uncomfortable, no one else will be, either. Even if you make a huge mistake, your ability to stay cool, calm, and collected is what they will remember.

How a Professional Can Help

In truth, even professional public speakers continue to work on their game. The rest of us can benefit greatly from a public speaking course or coach that will help you work through any anxieties.

Not only will you emerge from such an experience with more confidence, but you'll gain tips on how to better persuade or interest a crowd. A class will give you a safe place to practice giving speeches, helping you firm up an important aspect of speech-giving, practice and preparation.

A class will also allow you to speak with others who suffer from your same fear of speaking – your classmates. Hopefully, you'll begin to see how unfounded your fears really are, and you'll gain a friend or two in the meantime.

Your fears may seem like they're here to stay, but, as the saying goes, a person can get used to anything. Repetition is the key to quelling these anxieties, and soon you'll discover that, with a good attitude and a little effort, you'll be able to deliver an effective speech along with the best of them.

CHAPTER 5

The Arts of Persuasion and Negotiation

Persuasion is the art of convincing others to take your view and negotiation is the road you take to come to an acceptable agreement. If you've been in business for a while, you already know that these two interpersonal skills are rather indispensible.

When you have enhanced negotiation skills, you will be able to do the following:

- Understand or be willing to discover the root of whatever conflict or issue arises
- Listen attentively to those involved in the negotiation process
- Come to a conclusion about the viability of a proposed solution
- Be willing to come to an agreement that benefits everyone involved
- Come to a compromise, especially on small issues
- Be able to identify the most important issues

After you are learned in the art of persuasion, you will be better able to do the following:

- Present yourself or your argument in a flattering light to colleagues and coworkers
- Help others to understand your perspective
- Build rapport and strengthen relationships
- Show clients that you are in it to win it – together

Speak with Passion

Find your inner enthusiasm for your ideas, projects, and products, and others will, too. Excitement and enthusiasm are the kind of bugs that people *want* to catch. Not only that, but your evident passion will lend to your sincerity, which will in turn heighten your credibility.

When you're trying to bring someone over to your side or negotiate a better deal for your company, the last thing you want to do is be a bore. Keep your partners, clients, and colleagues awake and they will be better able to bring their own resolutions to the table.

Persuasion and negotiation tactics aren't all about you – sometimes people may surprise you, making you a better offer than even you thought possible. Stay enthusiastic, but keep an open mind pointed at those around you.

Follow up. Be Available

The acts of negotiation and persuasion aren't finished when the meeting ends or an agreement is reached. The lines of communication must remain open so that both parties can ensure their needs are met.

After a contract is signed and both parties know what they are in for, it's beneficial to establish a follow-up process. By going through these motions, both groups will be able to gain a clear understanding of how the agreement served to benefit them – or not. Both kinds of feedback will allow your company to better access its ability to persuade, negotiate, and, most importantly, follow through.

Be First to End the Meeting

Structure is an important aspect of business meetings. Each gathering should have a well-established beginning and end time; extending a meeting for too long a period can strain company offers and irritate attendees, who likely have a hundred other things to do.

Meetings, however, are often held in order to establish some kind of agreement. Being the first to bring the meeting to a close can be an effective negotiation tactic, as long as you play your cards correctly. Ending the meeting will give you an air of power, and perhaps make you something of a hero in the eyes of those who have 500 other things to do today.

To end a meeting without forestalling the purpose of the gathering, use the following techniques:

- **Note the Time:** When the allotted time has run its course, it's time to take a step back. If no agreement has been made, suggest everyone think it over and reconvene later.

- **Know When to Quit:** If you see a deadlock coming, don't spend the next hour arguing with people who can't be persuaded. Call time.
- **Set up a Series:** Like baseball, some sports are better hashed out over a series of games. Learn to recognize when more than one meeting is required to establish a potential agreement.
- **Announce an Agreement:** When all parties have managed to reach a conclusion, don't hang around any longer than necessary. If your plans are made, the meeting is over.

Understand Your Subject Matter

When it comes to persuasion and negotiation, the benefits that go along with an understanding of your subject matter are undeniable. It's simple, really: If your audience can't understand what you're talking about, they won't be persuaded. If you don't know what you're talking about, you can't illuminate them.

The benefits of being an authority on your topic are more than just fundamental. When you are able to present yourself as someone who has done extensive research or gained enough experience, you create a foundation of credibility. This credibility will lend itself to trust, and that trust will allow you to create rapport and build relationships. All of this starts with knowledge. In the case of persuasion, knowledge truly is power.

Understand Your Audience

Before you can begin persuading or negotiating, you must take the time to learn all you can about your subjects. Although most psychologists agree that there are only a few personality types, there is a myriad of exterior and interior factors that influence each person in different ways, resulting in countless communication styles and reactions to those styles.

Since you don't want your subject to respond aggressively to the communication style you've selected, it's a good idea to get a picture of what they're about before you meet on important matters.

Getting to know other people can be a simple matter of asking the right questions. As you don't want your counterpart to feel like the subject of an interrogation, be sure to do so in a conversational way. Find out what a potential client likes to do, what he doesn't. Express an interest in where he comes from and his personal background. Discover his hopes for the future and what he hopes to achieve in his career.

When you approach your subject in this kind of business-free manner – say, during a game of golf – you're improving your chances at persuading him to like your views or to sign a coveted contract. Engaging your subject in such a way is ideal for three reasons:

- The more he talks, the more he opens up to you.
- He is likely to notice your interest and feel respected and acknowledged.

- The knowledge you gain from this experience will better leverage your chances to negotiate and persuade because you are unraveling his real wants and needs. These desires provide important clues about how to proceed without offending.

Let's look at the example of Eva, a saleswoman whose main source of income was based on the art of persuasion. Early on, she was able to enhance her game with the realization that not everyone was dying to hear about a product's benefits and features.

Rather, she began to practice a question-based sales technique. When she approached a subject, instead of immediately expounding upon the benefits of her product, she simply asked him a few questions to begin. When she had a clear idea of what he both wanted and needed in a product, she was better able to recommend a solution. Not only that, but she could tell him precisely what he wanted to hear about the product rather than presenting a generic list of features.

Rapport: What You Need to Know

A sense of rapport between two people indicates that they trust and are comfortable with each other. It can be tricky to cultivate, since we don't always make rational decisions about whom we like or dislike.

When you build rapport and, subsequently, establish better relationships, your company benefits in more ways than one. Naturally, the rapport you've helped create with clients and customers will contribute directly to business, but it will also spread. When someone leaves your business as a happy customer, that happy customer is likely to spread the word of your good services and contribute to word-of-mouth advertising for your company.

How do you build rapport? Start at the beginning.

Building Rapport through Conversation

When you meet a new client or potential investor, begin the ritual of rapport-building with a little light, friendly conversation. Search for common interests by inquiring about the usual suspects – hobbies, extracurricular activities, common acquaintances, or places traveled. Discovering a common passion will really help you bring out the best in people.

If you fail to elicit the kernels of rapport right away, consider how your subject is communicating. People generally communicate via three different styles:

- **Auditory Style:** Those who use this style will generally use the phrases "I hear what you are saying," "Tell me more," and "That sounds familiar."

- **Visual Style:** These people like to say things like "I see what you mean," "I can imagine," and "I get the picture."

- **Kinesthetic Style:** Favorite phrases for those who utilize kinesthetic style include things like "I need solid evidence," "I get the feeling that..." and "Give me some solid facts."

When you can't connect with a subject, it may simply be that you are using different communication styles. Rather than giving up, try to approach communication their way. If they need facts, supply them. If they need to hear your version of events, speak up. If they need to picture what you're saying, be more descriptive.

Use Body Language to Your Benefit

Remember that a large part of our message is communicated via body language. If you're not getting along with others, it may not be what you're saying. Rather, you may have to adjust your body's response to a group setting.

Remember the aspects of open, positive body language and use them when you hope to persuade or negotiate. More than the words you speak, focus on how your voice *sounds* to other people. Often displaying your interest and openness through body language is all you need to better your relationships.

Be Subtle

Too much enthusiasm may be interpreted as aggression, which, when it comes to persuasion, is the opposite of helpful. Likewise, you don't want to mirror your subject's every move. Rather than building rapport, you may just make him uncomfortable. Don't fake happiness or enthusiasm when you don't feel it; doing so might make you seem fake or even a bit psychotic.

Be open, but don't reveal too much. Be friendly without being overeager. Be interested without appearing desperate. Strike the perfect balance and you can't help but succeed.

Visualize a Promising Future

When we meet an important client, it's only natural to feel a bit jittery. To insulate those nerves, take a moment before you head to the big meeting or annual fundraiser and practice positive visualization.

Imagine meeting this important client and winning him over. See yourself approaching him smoothly and striking up a conversation. Visualize you making plans for a game of golf, a lunch appointment, or setting a time to mull over a contract. Imagine the best possible of all outcomes and visualize it. You'll be surprised at how positive an outcome you can create for yourself when it's time to starting building rapport.

CHAPTER 6

Be Heard: Assertion Tactics for Better Business

Nurture Your Company with Assertive Practices

Before you begin practicing your new assertive ways, it's important to differentiate between assertion and other, less ideal ways to communicate.

- **Assertion:** When you act assertively, you make yourself understood in a professional manner that is respectful to others.

- **Aggression:** Those who act aggressively are coming from a place of demand and dominance.

- **Passivity:** Those who communicate passively show that they are receptive to outside influences and readily agree with others.

Assertive communication techniques are ideal for use in more than just the workplace. When you act assertively, you let others know where you are coming from without infringing on their personal space or feelings. You also clearly state what you really mean or want without letting others crush your needs with their own opinions and desires.

To become assertive, there are a few things you must take into consideration.

Timing Is Everything

More than knowing exactly what you wish to say, it's important to know when to say it. This little nugget is even more important in the world of business. It is essential to time your messages properly, as not being able to do so is likely to diminish your professional credibility. Speaking up when you should keep silent can be as damaging as remaining quiet when you should be speaking up. So how can we deduce that the right time has come?

In a group setting, make sure to allow a pause after someone has finished speaking. This way, you ensure that you won't be speaking over anyone, which can be interpreted as rude and has the additional detriment of clogging the lines of effective communication.

When you are invited to speak, don't hesitate. An invitation can be subtle – perhaps your colleague has drifted into silence and is looking at you expectantly. Now is the time to share your perspective.

But when do you keep your thoughts to yourself? One way of ascertaining whether or not you should pipe up is to take note of the moods of others in the group. If they seem especially irritable today, it may not be the right time to tackle the most controversial issue in the office.

It's also a good idea to edit your thoughts so that you're only sharing essential information. Talking too much can be as problematic as speaking at the wrong moment. In order to ensure everyone stays interested in what you have to say, only share the information worth sharing.

Impromptu business sessions shouldn't take longer than a few minutes. By stretching them beyond what is necessary, you are costing your coworkers precious minutes that they could be putting to good use. Not only that, but it shouldn't take long to resolve an issue that prompts an unplanned meeting.

If you find a planned meeting has surpassed the allotted time, stop and consider whether you're still discussing important topics or if your time could be spent more productively.

Choose Your Words Wisely

When your aim is to express assertiveness, word choice becomes all-important. Assertive-style communication relies upon the self, whereas aggressive style is all about the other person. Of course, it's important not to appear self-involved, either.

An assertive statement begins with an I-statement and goes on to include others. For example: "It seems to me that we should meet around noon. I'd like to know if that works for everyone," or, "I believe this report is outdated. What do you think?"

You are firmly stating your position, but, as you bring others into the statement, you create openness and encourage freedom of expression.

Assertive language gets to the point quickly, keeping adverbs and adjectives to a minimum, and utilizing shorter word. It is applied in sentences of twenty words or less. Unless someone else requests further information, it's not necessary to divulge all the unnecessary details.

"Cindy, it's important that I have your spreadsheet by noon tomorrow" is an assertive statement.

A less assertive version might go something like this: "Cindy, you know that spreadsheet of vital statistics that I requested yesterday? If it's alright with you, I need that by tomorrow sometime, preferably in the morning."

In the assertive statement, no time is wasted as Cindy is informed what you need from her. In the longer, passive statement, Cindy is receiving the same request, but the speaker's choice of words sends a mixed message.

Assertive Body Language

As with all of our other modes of communication, body language plays a huge part in assertiveness. Again, a huge portion of what we mean is perceived by others through our body language – no matter what you say, people are going to respond largely to how they see you. By making the right moves – displaying confident posture, relaxed facial expressions – people will see you as assertive rather than aggressive or passive.

The same kinds of body language that make you appear friendly and open to others will also give people the idea that you are assertive. With your shoulders back, head up, palms open, arms relaxed, and feet shoulder-width apart, people will not only feel that they are free to do business with you, they'll know that you mean business as well.

As you probably remember, we can't completely control our body language, but, with a little self-awareness and some practice, we can ensure that we are communicating the necessary amount of assertion. All interpersonal skills rely heavily upon the choices we make with our body language, so it is counterproductive to leave these choices up to our bodies.

10 Steps to Ideal Assertiveness

1. Assert control over your own assertiveness. By making the conscious decision to become more assertive, you'll be able to stay in the moment and make better communication choices.

2. Remain open and honest. Get to the point about what you really want in an honest manner, but show people that you respect them at the same time. People will extend the same privilege to you.

3. Exercise active listening skills. Assert your point of view, but don't forget that others have one, too (see chapter on being an active listener).

4. It's okay to disagree. Often, exercising assertive communication skills means that you are putting your disagreement on the table. It doesn't have to mean that you are right and everyone else is wrong. It does mean, however, that there are many more opinions and perspectives than your own.

5. Don't let others make you feel guilty. If Cindy needs to turn in her spreadsheet, there's no reason for you to feel guilty about asking for it – Cindy is getting paid to create spreadsheets. Likewise, don't make others feel guilty when they come to you with assertive statements of their own.

6. Keep calm. Keeping your cool in a tough situation is the best way to keep negative emotions from taking over. Calm collectedness makes up much of the foundation of positive interpersonal skills.

7. Approach problems with solutions, not emotions. By initiating problem-solving techniques, you keep yourself from cultivating bad personal feelings for another person. Attack an issue, not a person.

8. Practice, practice, practice. Make assertive statements in the mirror or at home with someone you trust. This way, you get a feel for them, and they arise naturally when you have a need for them.

9. Remember to say "I" not "you." Always begin your statement with phrases like "I think" or "I feel." When you begin by pointing out that "you always..." or "you never..." you cultivate defensiveness in the other person.

10. Practice some more. Don't beat yourself up if you don't become the world's most assertive boss on the first day. These skills take time to master, and some days may be better than others.

CHAPTER 7

Keep Business Running Smoothly With Effective Conflict Resolution

Workplace conflicts are often less damaging than what we normally think of when we hear the word conflict. However, just because these conflicts happen on a smaller scale than the Battle of the Bulge, it doesn't mean that they can't be complicated in their own way.

Conflicts arise whenever two or more people or groups have some kind of disagreement that threatens personal ideas surrounding needs, concerns, or interests. A conflict could be as small as one person accusing another of finishing the coffee pot and not brewing more coffee. Even a minor conflict can ruin a workday if it isn't handled correctly.

Manage Conflicts Effectively for Better Business

When two fully formed personalities meet and exist together for a prolonged period of time, some form of conflict is inevitable. Most disturbances are no big deal, but all must be resolved in a productive manner.

This is vital to keeping business running smoothly.

If workplace conflict becomes drawn out, it can affect other employees, effectively souring the office mood and potentially putting off clients and customers. Since interpersonal skills are an important aspect of doing business, it's important to keep them sharp. One way to do this is through conflict resolution.

Even if you are personally involved in the conflict, you must consider all sides of all issues before deciding how to move forward.

Conflicts are best resolved in a way that is fair and beneficial for all parties. Sometimes it takes a third, uninvolved party to step in and moderate the conflict resolution. This person can take a nonbiased view and help everyone see a better way toward a resolution.

To effectively resolve a conflict, it's necessary to understand the people behind the problem. What is the real issue here? What do these people need, believe, or presume? Since injured personal beliefs, needs, or desires are often at the root of such a disagreement, it's important to understand them.

How to Manage Conflict

Use Assertive Communication Skills

Now that you're learning how to master the ways of assertive communication, you know the difference between this and aggressive communication. Recall that aggressive communication is often turned on the other person in the form of an accusation or other hurtful phrase.

When you use assertive communication, you are asserting strong, firm language over the situation. There's no better use for assertion than in conflict resolution, since it can be used to make statements without creating hurt feelings.

For example, if a late employee has created a conflict with his absence, you can use assertive language to handle the situation: "I see that you didn't come in on time today. It's important for all of us to be here at 9:00 a.m., otherwise our ability to do business may be jeopardized. Please come in on time from now on."

Rather than accusing the employee of purposely thwarting business practices or of being selfish, this assertive statement makes an impact without getting personal. In other words, it solves a problem without creating negative emotions, which could make that employee feel defensive and further hinder business practices.

Remember that if you need to manage a conflict, it's best to do so in a constructive manner.

Set Healthy Boundaries

Each of us has need of a set of healthy personal boundaries, at the workplace as well as anywhere else. To establish yours, you need to know what you will and won't put up with in terms of conflict. Your boundaries are made up of that tolerance, and when those boundaries are crossed you must have a plan of action. It sounds simple, but to set boundaries, first we must get to know ourselves.

We understand ourselves better with experience, and the same goes for our boundaries. As we go through experiences that make us uncomfortable or unhappy, we learn where our boundaries lie. As we mature or our lifestyle changes, our boundaries often change at the same time.

You can have all the boundaries you want, but they won't mean anything if you can't communicate them to other people. Here, again, is where your new assertive skills will come in handy.

Understanding Before All Else

As we learn more about ourselves, it will become easier to spot our own role in each conflict. There are two ways to do so.

The first is to consider how you ended up in the conflict in the first place. Did it begin with you? Was it something you said or did? What could you have done differently to avoid the entire predicament?

The second method involves seeing the conflict from another perspective – that is, to imagine how the other person sees it. Who is this person? What does he have to deal with on a daily basis? Why is he behaving this way? If you spoke to him directly about the conflict, would he be able to control or confront his behavior? Should you exercise compassion rather than blame?

Conflict begins and ends with us. It's up to us to resolve our differences in a peaceful and effective manner, especially when these differences arise in the workplace.

To work toward resolution, we must examine ourselves and the role we play in each conflict. If we are constantly surrounded by problems, it's safe to assume that it's time to rethink the way we are doing business.

By using assertive communication skills, committing to healthy boundaries, and working toward an understanding of others, we can resolve or reduce any tough conflict that might arise at work. It will take a bit of work, but as you improve these skills, you'll establish healthier relationships even as you work your way out of conflicts.

Problematic Situations and Their Resolutions

The methods of conflict resolution can be applied to conflicts in any walk of life. Keeping with our business theme, let's take a look at a couple of possible workplace conflict scenarios and how they should be resolved.

The Conflict: Billy, who was forced to deal with a personal crisis early in the morning, making him late for work, has arrived at the office feeling pressured to make up for lost time. Normally an energetic, fast-talking guy, he is especially on edge today.

Mary, one of Billy's clients, is a sweet Southern gal who tends to take life much slower than Billy. Billy knows from experience that he has to tone down his natural personality in his dealings with her, but when she calls today, he overdoes it, and Mary feels that he is patronizing her and becomes frustrated. Billy can hear in Mary's voice that she's becoming defensive, a fact that is fueling his own defensiveness.

The Solution: Billy would be wise to postpone his conversation with Mary until he feels less pressured.

When he asks to postpone their business dealing, Mary will understand that Billy isn't having the best day and would be less irritable and better able to deal with her later.

If Mary requires services right away, then both need to consider the other's schedule and stress level. Mary must work to disregard Billy's tone of voice, dismissing her personal feelings in favor of doing urgent business.

The Conflict: Kerry, the manager, has been putting off a meeting she needs to have with one of her employees, Tim. Kerry needs to tell Tim that he's been too agreeable and not at all decisive enough. She fears that her meeting with him will be time-consuming and, by the end of it, nothing will be achieved.

Tim is anticipating the conversation with equal dread. Kerry never listens to him, constantly interrupting and never letting him fully explain his point of view. When this happens, he becomes incredibly uncomfortable and starts to wish she would just tell him what to do and how to do it.

As Kerry becomes more and more impatient with Tim, she begins to talk over him more, and, increasingly, Tim says less and less. Kerry thinks that Tim is weak, and Tim sees Kerry as intimidating.

The Solution: Kerry and Tim's opposing behaviors feed each other in terms of negativity, and neither one perceives exactly what is happening.

Both need to focus more on their own behavior and withdraw blame from the other person.

Kerry should try to understand that when she talks over Tim, she sounds overbearing and angry. If she were paying attention, she would be able to see by Tim's body language that she is making him uncomfortable.

Tim needs to consider how is body language is being interpreted by Kerry. Instead of withdrawing, he needs to straighten his spine, look Kerry in the eye, and calmly tell her the information she needs to hear. Instead of wishing Kerry would like him as a friend, he should work to gain her respect as an employee.

Resolving conflict often takes our entire arsenal of interpersonal skills, and it may not come easy at first. Developing self-awareness in addition to an awareness of how we are being perceived takes work – work that may not be pleasant at first.

However, the payoff is incredible. Bigger business, better relationships, improved personal life and attitude are all things we can expect to achieve as we master these all-important people skills.

About The Author

Melissa Contreras – MBA, author, book publisher and online entrepreneur - understands the importance of using the right people skills to maximize business performance. Her passion for this subject matter led her to create two websites – Effective Communication Advice and Interpersonal Skills Online – to help others sharpen their people skills in a corporate kind of way. These websites receive hundreds of visitors per day.

   After thirteen years of working in corporate finance, commercial and multilateral banking, Melissa decided it was time to pursue her entrepreneurial goals and put her knowledge of the professional business environment into print, becoming a writer and online publisher. Always one to embrace change, she's lived in four countries – the U.S., U.K, Brazil, and Venezuela – and speaks four languages – English, Spanish, Portuguese, and French.

Her interest in multimedia enterprises has led her to begin her own book publishing business, helping entrepreneurs and small businesses create new opportunities for lead generation, establish their authority in their local industry and gain a competitive advantage.

If you are serious about improving the results of your business and would like to schedule a free consultation to see how Melissa can help you become a business authority, increase your clientele and take a bigger cut of the market share, you can contact her by sending her an email at www.ChestnutHillWriting.com or www.Melissa-Contreras.com

And if you'd like to learn more about polishing up your Interpersonal Skills, visit:

- InterpersonalSkillsOnline.com
- EffectiveCommunicationAdvice.com.

These sites offer extensive communication tips for business leaders, training methods and further reading on the subject. Those who'd like to brush up on their public speaking and presentation skills will also find these sites incredibly useful.